Cathy was brought up in North Cornwall on the family farm. Together she and her sisters had ponies on loan during the winter months and later had horses of their own. They spent many hours galloping across beaches and enjoying the fun of attending Pony Club Camp on Bodmin Moor.

Having left school, Cathy trained to teach riding before starting college. During that time, she became groom to the Junior Equestrian Team GB. She enjoys teaching and has supported many people over the years of all ability. She has thoroughly enjoyed helping her grandson, Matt, with his first pony, Pandora.

Cathy Mayes.

MATT AND PANDORA

Cathy Mayes

AUSTIN MACAULEY PUBLISHERS™
LONDON • CAMBRIDGE • NEW YORK • SHARJAH

Copyright © Cathy Mayes (2021)

A CIP catalogue record for this title is available from the British Library.

ISBN 9781528988292 (Paperback)
ISBN 9781528988308 (ePub e-book)

www.austinmacauley.com

First Published (2021)
Austin Macauley Publishers Ltd
25 Canada Square
Canary Wharf
London
E14 5LQ

To my parents who offered me the experience of riding, having ponies on loan and then owning my own horses, from childhood. They gave me the opportunity to go away and train to teach horse-riding, taking my love of horses to the next level.

To my wonderful family and friends for supporting my writing and giving continuous inspiration.

To Matt for being a 'star' and of course, Pandora!

To Mark Bernstein who has illustrated the story beautifully.

Chapter 1
The New Arrival

Anyone who has ever owned their own pony or horse will understand how Matt is feeling!

The day has come when my seven-year-old grandson may meet his new best friend. Matt has been interested in riding for a few years now and has been attending local riding schools for about two years. He has been riding and taking part in the Saturday club, where the children learn about stable management. He also attended summer camp last year, riding well-schooled ponies. Last week, Matt headed up to Wales with his mum, Lucy, and his auntie to see some ponies. It seems that Pandora was the first pony they visited, and Matt, along with Lucy and his aunt, fell in love immediately. The family tradition of ponies and horses continues!

The tradition of horses in the family goes back many years. My grandfather (Bam Bam) who lived in Somerset, used to use horses on the farm for ploughing, combining, threshing and general farm work. Elaine and Philip's gran used to deliver milk with a pony and cart, delivering milk from a tin can dipped into the milk churn which sat on the back of the trap, so that local people had fresh milk. I have recently found out that my great-great grandfather was a coachman at Bodrhyddan Hall, having started off as a groom and probably a stable boy before that. My sisters and I went to pony club and always enjoyed the camp during the summer holidays. After school, I went and worked with horses for a couple of years in Cirencester and looked after event and dressage horses. I went as a groom to Aachen in Germany with members of the junior and senior British dressage team. We attended many big events, such as Winsor Horse Show, Badminton, Burghley, Horse of the Year Show and many more. I completed my assistant instructors exams. Teaching riding has been something that I have done a lot over the years, teaching beginners right up to eventers, and I am delighted that I can now help my grandson to progress with his pony.

When my sisters and I were children, we learnt to ride at a stable near Yelverton, on the moors in Devon. Once we had moved to Cornwall, when I was ten years old, we used to have ponies on loan from the trekking centre over winter, at that time, the centre was run from our farm. We already knew the ponies very well and they knew us. Interesting though, how different ponies behave when they are not simply following the one in front, particularly, when they are faced with the expanse of beach or open field! Together with our ponies, we had many adventures. Mum and Dad both rode, Mum had ridden quite a lot in her earlier life, Dad learnt later in life and continued into his seventies, he always said that riding out was a great way to see what other farmers were doing with their crops and stock, looking over the top of the hedges. Two of my children, Elaine and Philip, learnt to ride when they were young, Philip was perhaps slightly more confident, they both attended Saturday club at the riding school. Whilst Elaine enjoyed riding and has hacked out with friends since, Philip has not really had much opportunity to continue riding. Elaine had a Shetland pony when she was about eighteen months old and I bought a wicker saddle for him, the top was more like a basket and Elaine could sit comfortably with her legs through the gaps in the basket. My youngest son, John, did not have riding lessons, although he has been on a hack with me when we holidayed in Ireland one year.

From that first day when Matt and Pandora met, there was no stopping him, all the conversations were about Pandora, what he would do with her in respect of looking after her, things they would do together, where he would take her, which stable she would have, how often he would ride. Non-stop excitement, so enamoured and longing to have her at home. Matt drew pictures of her, how he remembered her from his first visit and I had to print off three copies, then he realised looking back at photos that his mum had from the initial visit, that he had not given her four white socks, so more pictures, more printing, using a model horse to get the proportions and shape, with my help, though he may have done better on his own.

Today is the day! Just three days after the initial visit, and his aunt brought Pandora down to her new home, here in Cornwall. The first night Pandora stayed at her house, as Matt's cousin's horse was also in the horsebox coming home from an event. Matt, of course, went to stay for the night so that he could be close to his new pony. The first day they had together was very busy for everyone. Matt groomed and rugged Pandora on several occasions during the day! A new bridle had been bought and fitted, a saddle was on loan from his aunt and the pony was ridden three times that day. If there had been the opportunity, I think Matt would have slept out in the stable with her. I can remember spending many hours in the stable with my first horse, Bentley, my very own horse that is. Like Pandora, he was young, a three-year-old, though I was eleven, maybe twelve perhaps when I had him. I can remember that thrill, the excitement, the dreams and plans we made together in the stable and when we were out riding.

Matt is a boy who is passionate about his riding, keen and excited, caring and kind to his pony. He chats to his pony, tells her secrets, shares his news and excitements with her and tells her he loves her. They walk around the farm together, ride together and chat away in the stable. Whilst looking for a gift for Matt to celebrate the arrival of his new pony, I have noticed that a great deal of merchandise for children with ponies is targeted at girls. Pretty pink t-shirts with ponies on the front, pink grooming kits, and so on. In many pony-riding story books, there are the occasional boys, though the main characters are frequently girls. I do not have an issue with pinks, it is that I have not found any t-shirts, for example, with boys and their ponies or without sparkles and sequins. It seems that there are few designs with simply a horse or pony.

Perhaps we should have a bit more equality here, especially given some of our top horse riders are men, along with many top women riders across the world. So, there is a challenge for someone!

Having spent the first night and day with his pony at his aunt's and with his cousin plaiting her for him and making her look even more beautiful, Pandora finally arrived home to the farm where Matt and the rest of his family live. Beth, Matt's older sister, and Lucy had cleaned out the stable; Dan, his older brother, and Philip, his dad, had cleared the empty chicken runs to the side of the paddock and everyone including grandma had helped to make sure there was no rubbish in the field that could cause any possible damage or injury to the pony. Later in the summer, they will need to keep an eye out for ragwort which is prolific around here and poisonous to horses and ponies, especially in the early stages of growth before the bright yellow flowers emerge.

Pandora spent her first night in her new home in her own stable, with a calf next door for company; Matt did sleep in his own bed and, I expect, dreamt of all the things he and Pandora would do together.

The pony is indeed very pretty; she is a light, bright bay, with four long white socks, a predominantly white face, one wall-eye (a blue eye) and one black eye. She is Welsh Section A, about 11.2hh (each hand measuring approximately 10cms) and just the right size for Matt to be able to groom, tack up, put rugs on and to mount by himself. He may need some help to start with, though it will not be long before he is off by himself, looking at sheep for Philip and riding off around the fields. The pony is young, fairly 'green' (inexperienced) and unschooled, she is four years old and so they have plenty to learn together. Matt has learnt a lot of horsemanship at the riding schools he has attended and is quite confident with the care that his pony will require.

Having settled his pony for the night in her own stable, Matt planned his first day at home with his new best friend.

Everyone is very busy on the farm as it is lambing time of the year and the ewes need to be checked regularly; new lambs need to be caught and tagged as they are born, to ensure they stay with their own mothers and are not taken on by ewes that are still due to lamb. Beth and Dan both help on the farm, with lambing, checking sheep and tractor driving. Lucy is also busy working today as she looks after a property and needs to make it ready for new visitors arriving today. Philip and Lucy also have two delightful shepherd's huts on the farm which are let to holiday makers and require cleaning and maintenance between visitors. Today Lucy has asked me to come over and help Matt to do what he wants to do with the pony and to go with him for his ride. When I arrived, Matt had already groomed Pandora, twice apparently, and Beth had helped him to get the saddle on. We go down to the stable, the pony is busy munching on some hay and apparently tried a little munch on Matt's arm whilst they were putting the saddle on, she had not broken the skin and whilst it had pinched, Matt was fine.

I showed Beth and Matt that the saddle was a little too far back and so we took it off and I showed them where to place it whilst also pulling the numnah up into the tree of the saddle so that it did not stretch across the withers making it uncomfortable for the pony. I then put the bridle on and showed Matt and Beth how to measure the cheek-strap and the noseband to ensure the fit was correct and comfortable.

These are things that both Beth and Matt will soon do automatically, and I was simply re-enforcing what they knew. Practice is the thing. Matt will struggle with the saddle for a while, simply because of the weight of lifting it higher than the pony to position it properly, though it will not be long before he will do all these things for himself.

Once tacked up, Beth led Pandora up the lane to the house as Matt had gone up to collect his riding hat, body protector and put his jodhpur boots on. The farm is nestled down in a dip and surrounded by the fields, the lane is fenced on both sides, with sheep grazing quietly and new-born lambs running and bouncing about in playful mood. Wild flowers grow along the banks all the way up to the shepherd huts. We led the pony up the lane towards the huts, having closed the gate behind us to ensure that the area was safe from unexpected people or vehicles. Matt wanted to lead Pandora up to the end of the lane so that she knew the environment around her, when we got up the end of the lane to where visitors park their cars, Matt was given a leg-up by Beth. He did several rides up and down the lane, some walking, some trotting, getting used to his new pony. Matt managed very well, turning around, using his legs and voice to keep her trotting, it was hard work to keep her trotting, she kept going back to a walk. Being young, the pony responds well to the voice and is keen to listen to Matt's aids. The lane is not straight and so it was good practice for Matt with turning and using his legs to show the pony which way he wanted her to go. Matt used his inside leg on the girth and his outside leg behind the girth to turn his pony and was careful with his hands, opening out his rein rather than pulling her around. Using the inside and outside leg differently is something that Matt needs to practice, though he already has the right idea. We agreed that it would not be a good idea for Pandora to be ridden in the same place every day, and so next time, we will use the other lane on the farm that heads down towards the pond. There is a big grassy area along the lane and Matt made sure that the pony did not take it in her head to stop there for a little snack, though she tried.

Matt and Pandora went off to a pony club event on Sunday and enjoyed themselves having a lesson and fun and games with other children and ponies. The pony was not too keen on the baton being passed to Matt in one of the relay games and Matt landed on the ground, however, the pony stood still, Matt got up, brushed himself down and got on again, both enjoying the rest of the day. Matt also came home with a pony club badge for plaiting, so that was a good start to having fun together.

Today was the last day of the Easter holidays, the children all return to school tomorrow. Matt and I have agreed that I shall give him a lesson every Wednesday after school and then go and help on any other days that he needs help. I can see we are going to be very busy!

Chapter 2
Lessons Begin

Wednesday arrived. Arrangements had been made for today to be the weekly riding lesson day and the neighbours kindly agreed to loan us their sand school for these lessons. I had my instructions from Matt to be at the farm by four o'clock to help him prepare Pandora for his lesson due to start at five o'clock, so naturally I arrived at the given time, he was so keen, it was wonderful! Matt had brought in his pony to the stable, as the pony was in the small paddock during the day, he had already groomed her and picked out her feet to remove any stones that may have become stuck alongside the frog (the softer V-shaped area under the hoof) as soon as he came home from school. He was ready to tack up. Lucy, his mum, went to get the saddle and bridle from the workshop, she put the saddle on, and I then put the bridle on, soon we would be redundant for these jobs. Having tacked up, Matt put on his riding hat and body-protector. Together we walked Pandora up the lane to the shepherd huts, this was a safe and familiar place to start from and enclosed. Matt used the hedge as a mounting block to get on. He walked and trotted down the lane and then we walked up the main farm lane to get to the sand school next door. There were still stems from the clusters of beautiful yellow daffodils that had waved their heads in wind, been knocked back by snow and brightened again on sunny days. Rabbits sometimes run across the lane from the field to delve into their burrows in the hedge. We are grateful to have permission to use the sand school for the lessons, now that the fields are saturated from a winter of what seemed like torrential rain, and it is no good just cutting them up with riding, also as the pony is not shod, we do not want to always be using the lanes which are stony and hard for her feet.

Matt wanted to be on the lead rein to walk up the main lane as it comes up to a road that can become quite busy, particularly, at this time of the year with holiday makers and farmers. It is best to move at the child's pace and not to push them into things that they are not confident about as it simply stirs fear and anxiety which are not a good combination with horses or ponies. I am aware that Matt will tell me when he feels confident and wants to leave the lead rein behind. As it happened, the lead rein was a good thing, there were a lot of vehicles coming and going on the farm today, and as we came near the top of the lane, Matt's dad, Philip, appeared with the tractor and a full load of round bales on a very noisy rattling trailer, black and pink plastic flying from the round bales where it had become snagged on the hedges along the narrow lanes. The pony was amazing and whilst she was clearly nervous, she just backed towards the fence slightly with me holding her. I told Matt that everything was okay and told him to just relax, keep his heels down and bottom down in the saddle, he appeared far more relaxed than I think he felt, this helped the pony to relax. We walked behind the tractor and down the parallel lane to the sand school. There were various potential hazards for such a young pony with this new environment; there were horses in stables, whinnying and kicking at the doors, chickens wandering around, a dog barking, and whilst I did not see them on the way in, I noticed a few pigs in a pen, when we were leaving. With my own young horse, the smell of the pigs would have been enough to have him bolt back down the lane to his stable, he hated pigs.

Pandora whinnied to the horses and had a careful look around the school and at the whole new environment. I kept her on the lead rein whilst we checked out the school (it is an outdoor area), walking around on both reins (different directions) and in decreasing circles around the outside. I asked Matt if he was happy for me to take the lead rein off, he was happy at this point to do so. He worked hard to keep the pony going, using his voice and legs to encourage her.

Pandora would have been quite happy to follow me around the school rather than following Matt's aids. Young ponies need to be pushed on sometimes and yet we may assume that they will always be forward going. Matt kept his legs on and kept his seat down, just as well as he had to contend with a few small jumps as the pony spooked a little at the strange new sounds and smells around her. There are so many scary monsters that ponies conjure up in their heads.

There were some poles in the school as well as a jump which Lucy had put down for safety. Matt was very keen to get his pony over the poles, and so after we had a good warm up, I spaced them out so that she could walk over them, they did this on both reins. Matt trotted and walked on both reins and was pleased with what they had achieved together. It was important that this lesson was relaxed, safe and comfortable for Matt, otherwise he may not have been keen to come back another day, there is a lot to do and it is important that it happens at Matt and Pandora's pace. Today we had overcome scary monsters and potential hazards. Next time, we will get to work on skills and style. We left the school after about half an hour to walk back down the lane to the farm, no tractors this time, just Lucy in her car. Halfway down, I took the lead rein off and Matt walked the rest of the way on his own, dismounting near the house so that we did not need to negotiate any noisy monsters masquerading as tractors when we approached the yard! We walked down to the stable and took off the tack and made sure that Pandora had some hay and water for the night. Matt also made sure that she had no small stones in her feet from the lane. She will go out in the paddock in the morning. The pony has wood shavings in her stable and Matt needed to skip out some dung so that she had a comfortable bed for the night as she likes to lie down.

Matt enjoyed his first lesson and I would say that it went very well, a young pony and a young boy together enjoying each other's company and already getting in tune. There is a lot to learn and plenty of time and opportunity to learn together. Having fun is one of the most important aspects of riding, given caring for a pony and riding are both hard work and require total commitment. A good first lesson, especially given the potential hazards, added to which it was a very windy day and so there were plenty of bangs and noises going on around us.

Matt wanted some help so that he could ride after school a couple of days later, so not exactly a lesson as we are only going to use the sand school once a week, given the neighbours have been kind enough to offer it. So today is going to be a relaxed opportunity to just tweak some things and learn a few new pointers ready for Wednesday. Matt did not want to use the lead rein today and used the wall by the house as a mounting block rather than having a leg-up, he needs a little more spring for that! What we concentrated on today was a forward going walk and trot. I explained to Matt that he should use his legs alternately to get a forward going walk, he did not understand what I meant to start with, and so I stood in front of Pandora and showed him. I said to him 'Use this leg, now use that leg, use this one again, and so on'. So off he went saying 'one, two, one, two' and he found that the walk was more extended, comfortable and easier to keep the pony going. Having achieved a good walk, he made the transition to a trot and kept his pony trotting the full length of the lane, this

was the first time. Matt's face was beaming with pleasure and pride at achieving this, both the pony and
his confidence soaring.

We talked about meeting the tractor up the lane on our first visit to the sand-school, Matt was quite funny about the incident and he said that he had been VERY nervous and thought that he might fall off. 'That tractor is huge and scary for a small pony and for me even when I was on top of the pony and higher than her'. If I am honest I would say that we were all a little nervous, particularly because we know so little about what Pandora has experienced in her short life. Pandora was wonderful, and I never felt that there was a risk to their safety. Today there were two tractors in the yard, one was loading the feeder wagon and the other was hitched to the wagon, both had engines running. Philip was driving the quad to go and see sheep and he had a trailer on the back and there was also the farm truck. Whilst perhaps a little wary, the pony walked quietly passed it all. Matt said, "There is not much to scare Pandora now, she has seen all the tractors and, well, all the other stuff is in Wales as well, you know!'

Matt was so pleased with his riding today, getting Pandora to walk so well and then finding the transition to trot easier, he would like to ride for longer next time and do dressage! I explained that dressage is made of walk, trot, canter, halt, most of which he had achieved today, though we will work on a turn on the forehand and stepping backwards next time. With these skills, Matt will be able to open and close a gate without needing to dismount. Having learnt that, he will be closer to being able to go and check some sheep with his pony. Just now he is not too keen to canter, that will come as his confidence grows and we are going to start doing some exercises soon to help his seat get deeper in the saddle, and his legs to wrap around the pony, giving him more security.

Today has been a great success and Matt has been brimming with pride and pleasure during his ride and, on several occasions, has leaned forward and wrapped his arms around his pony's neck and patted her. When we were finished, I said to Matt he could go through the gate and wait for me, as I needed to push the gates open for people to be able to drive up to the shepherd huts. When I turned around, he had his feet out of his stirrups and his reins long and he looked so relaxed. It was lovely to see this, though I had to say that he must always think about safety for himself and his pony, especially with such a busy farm and several vehicles driving in and out. It was, however, a real pleasure to see this relaxed and happy exchange between pony and rider.

Chapter 3
First Hack

'Well, I had the best weekend ever,' said Matt. On Saturday, he went for a hack with his aunt and his cousin riding their horses and Lucy leading Matt on Pandora. This was a big adventure! From his aunt's house, they went through two fields, Pandora was 'rather keen' Lucy said. Ponies are like most animals, the sight of an open field full of green grass excites them, have you ever seen cattle when they are let out in to the field after being in the shed over the winter months, or new born lambs on a sunny spring day? It seems that the combination of grass, sunshine, space and freedom gives us all a spring in our step, Pandora is no different. Having passed through two green fields, they arrived at the road where they could ride around the block and back home to auntie's house.

On the road, Matt was happy to go off the lead rein and he was confident to ride on and trot with the others. We need to remember that for Matt and Pandora together this is all new and exciting. Individually, they have both been out for hacks before, but together this was a first and, for Lucy, I suspect, it was all quite nerve-wracking, we all want our children to be safe. The hack was a great success and had given Matt's confidence an additional boost.

Following the hack, Matt stayed over with his aunt and was apparently out in the sand school with his pony before going to rugby practice. I must admit he is keen! Later in the day whilst going over some poles in the sand school, he slipped off, was leaning a little far forward and ended up on the ground. No injury, no problem, just mounted again and on his way.

Our ride today was probably not as exciting as the hack, though we have a good routine going where the pony and Matt work together, feel safe and are honing their skills. Matt groomed his pony and I helped him to tack her up. There is a step now to use as a mounting block and Pandora came alongside with me holding her whilst Matt mounted, we really need to improve that spring to enable Matt to mount more easily and gently! We do not need the lead rein now, the pony takes little notice if any of the huge tractors and wagons, which once posed as monsters; she walks steadily through the yard and up towards the lane. I open the gates and close them behind us, and Matt and the pony go off down the lane towards the shepherd huts; in many ways, I am no longer needed for this ride. However, there is work and learning to be done and we use the opportunity to learn new skills in a relaxed and fun way. Turn on the forehand is on the agenda today and a good square halt. These two actions will help Matt when he wants to open a gate without dismounting.

First the warm up, a good walk, followed by an active trot, both sitting and rising. I need Matt to lengthen his legs around the pony, so we cross over his stirrups and do some exercises, firstly raising his knee and pushing his leg down; then knee up, push down with the other leg and finally do the exercise with both legs at the same time. This is both an easy and very effective exercise to get the legs and seat down. The next exercise is to move his legs from thigh to ankle forward and back, keeping it as straight as possible. This stretches the muscle and brings the leg into a good position, free from the constraints of stirrup leathers. We spend about five minutes on relaxing and stretching as they are things that

Matt can do anytime. With short, regular practice sessions, this will improve his position, giving him more security in the saddle. With stirrups back on and lengthened by two holes, we continue.

The extended walk is improving all the time and transition to trot is good, I would say both pony and rider are tired after their big adventure at the weekend and so tomorrow needs to be a day of rest for both, at least from riding. Having done some good work, we moved on as Matt is keen to bring his pony to a good square halt, he wants to get involved in dressage when he is an official pony club member. It is hard to explain that to get a good halt you need to ride the pony forward into it.

I explain the aids to Matt, and he looks perplexed, tries it anyway. The front feet are square, the back feet not quite, though I would say a good effort all round. The most important thing is that you must feel it. The pony will pivot on its front legs, moving its back legs around, and with Pandora being young, we are only looking at a 45 degree turn today. After each attempt, it is important to praise both pony and rider and to take the pony off for a good extended walk, followed by a trot and transition back to walk, this would loosen the pony up for their next attempt. Matt opened the gate at the end of our forty-minute ride and walked down to the yard on his pony. He did say that there would be some gates that he will have to dismount for as they need a bit of a lift and other gates, like the big metal gate where he will have to be careful about the metal spring bolts that stick out. He is being safety conscious and considering the welfare of his pony.

We took the pony into the stable, I removed the saddle and Matt the bridle. I went and got some hay and Matt filled the water bucket. The tack is returned to the workshop, the stable skipped out (dung removed in a trug) and the pony is settled for the night. Whilst these jobs are Matt's responsibility, it helps to have someone to help and also to model how to do certain things, like putting your hand under the mouth to take the bit, rather than it clanking on the teeth as it comes out of the mouth.

It will become clear to Matt that all the things he is learning whilst on or off his pony are part of building their partnership, learning together and using these transferable skills. Turn on the forehand is about understanding how to use your legs and hands to achieve a position, or move with your pony, not simply about being able to open a gate, as is a good square halt and being able to get your pony to walk a few strides backwards. These skills will also be required in pony club tests and dressage in the future.

Chapter 4
Tumble-Time

Today was a great achievement for Matt, despite landing on the ground in the sand school. The beginning of the hour's session began so well, and the ending was positive and happy. I had hurt my leg and it was very painful to walk, so I needed to drive my car up to the top of the farm lane and then walk down to the sand school with Matt. I watched Matt all the way up the lane using the mirrors and he rode Pandora very well, from the pony spooking at some invisible monster near the house and sitting tight to reaching the top of the lane. The neighbours who loan us the sand school were parked across the lane at the top and so all was safe and secure from any large vehicles trying to come down the lane towards Matt. I quickly parked my car so that I met Matt before he reached the top of the lane where traffic whizzes passed on our Cornish country lanes and before the neighbours moved away. They were very impressed at pony and rider doing that long stretch on their own. We walked alongside each other down to the sand school, being the independent type, I was not to lead the pony, and to be fair, it was not necessary.

This was only our second visit and, naturally, there were things to look at for the pony, again the horses were whinnying and kicking their stable doors, pigs were snorting and chickens flapping, dogs barking. Once again, it was a very windy day and even the white electric fence tapes were flapping about and catching the sun, giving them a glittery shine. Interestingly, the pony seemed to find the shadows very interesting this evening, we were later than last week as I had to collect my car from the garage after collecting the children from school. The sun was lower and the shadows longer, Pandora registered an interest in everything though continued walking around the school, clearly keeping an eye on the shadows following her about. We concentrated on ever-decreasing circles and then spiralling out and small circles around the edge of the school, this helps both pony and rider to focus on the riding rather than the hidden hazards of field life and also helps the pony to become more supple.

Having completed an excellent warm up including the initial walk up the long farm lane, as Matt pointed out, we started to do some extended walking and practised coming to a square halt. I had intended to do some work without stirrups today and continue with some new exercises, however, as they made the transition into the second trot, the pony spooked, not sure why or what had frightened her, unfortunately whilst Matt sat well and kept his hands down, he did fall off. He was not hurt though it was a heavy fall and I think, his body protector jarred his stomach a bit, and as happens to all of us, pride was dented, confidence wobbled. I made sure that he was uninjured, the pony was standing close by looking somewhat surprised at what had just happened. Once Matt stood up, he decided he did not want to get back on and I said that he needed to as it was too far for him to lead the pony home and that I would have to drive the car back down to the farm following him, as he had requested earlier. Matt is a tough cookie and true to form, he took a leg-up and re-mounted his pony. I made him laugh when I said we needed to do something about his 'spring' both for getting on the pony and so that he had a softer landing the next time he took a tumble!

Having re-mounted and played follow the leader after me, confidence returned, and it was suggested, very politely of course, that it was not necessary for pony and rider to follow me, they could manage the circles on their own and the spirals.

These exercises are hard work for a young pony who has clearly not had much schooling, it is also hard work for a young rider as he had to concentrate on his aids and not on what noises or monsters may spook the pony a second time. As the confidence rose in the daring duo, our hosts returned from seeing their other horses and were keen to ask Matt about his pony. I suggested that he showed them what he had been doing and off he went with more confidence and determination to show what he had achieved. A circle of trot on both reins followed by a steady, rather sedate trot on the long side of the sand school. Praise and acknowledgement does wonders for us all, however small it is, and thanks to our select audience, the session finished on a high for pony and rider.

We said thank you for the use of the school and set off back towards the top of the farm lane. As we walked along, relaxed and chatting together, we saw Lucy walking, rather striding towards us. Matt, like all young boys, was pleased to see his mum and his resolve wavered slightly. From the walk up the lane to returning the pony to the stable had taken an hour, so both pony and rider were ready for refreshment and rest. We continued to the top of the lane and Lucy walked alongside the intrepid pair on their journey down the long lane home. I collected my car and followed slowly behind. I could have gone on in front, though I felt it good practice for the pony to be followed at a safe distance by a car, as with going on hacks this is likely to happen, particularly at this time of the year with many visitors driving around our Cornish lanes. It was lovely to see Matt riding in a relaxed and confident manner, chatting away to Lucy, patting his pony and just walking on a long rein after a good and I expect tiring lesson for both. It is useful for me to observe my young rider in different ways, whilst teaching, and whilst chilled and relaxed, not realising he is being watched. He has a great position which already shows signs of improvement, he does not have to think all the time, heels down for example, he just does it, his seat is improving and getting deeper in the saddle and his hands are still soft and open. Halfway down the lane, there is a pull-in by a field gate and Lucy and Matt had stopped there for me to pass, so yet another experience of being passed by a car. This is all good and part of the learning process for pony and rider, preparing them for real situations when out on the roads and boosting confidence.

Whenever people take a fall, there is the chance of a dent

in their confidence. Matt is no different, and whilst he got back up on the pony, it is clear and understandable that he does not want to fall off again. There is something about the sand school that unsettles the pony, perhaps the other horses being around, the banging and crashing with the strong wind and the various flapping around the sides. These are all things that the pony needs to get used to, and she will. Matt needs to build his confidence and he needs to feel safe to ride his pony. The issue is that I am working with a pony that is young, green and unschooled and a young rider who is extremely keen, inexperienced and unskilled with a young pony.

The next move I have decided on is to lunge the pony in the sand school so that she gets used to the various hazards, this is good for her and will help her to become more confident with new experiences. Once the pony has been lunged then Matt can ride her on the lunge, both will begin to feel more confident together and we will be able to move forward again. At this stage, it is very important to work at the pony and the rider's pace. Causing anxiety to either party will not help us move forward, they are a team. There is no one else to ride the pony, given her size, and so they need to learn together, have fun and be safe.

The second tumble was on the hard, stony ground by the shepherd huts, the pony spooked at some black matting piled in the corner, no real reason for this other than it being another new experience for her. Matt picked himself up, he was a little shaky but picked up the reins and said to Pandora, 'It's okay, they are not going to hurt you.' He was not too keen to get straight back up, but we made a joke about how we would get his spring into action as we did not have a mounting block to help. Luckily, his dad came around the corner and lifted Matt straight up. We had intended to do some practice games today and so we did; just at a walk though. Pandora had been nervous of a baton at the last pony club event, and so we practised, Matt taking a baton from me and then returning it; we had taken some buckets out with us as well so that Matt could practise going in and out of the buckets. This takes his mind off the pony and helps him to think about his turns, looking where he is going and using his legs to turn the pony.

Amazingly, the pony did not stop and look for food in the buckets, though we had turned them upside down as she has quite an appetite. The tumble was soon forgotten, and we had a sedate lesson, working on the length of the reins, opening both reins out when the pony napped and using legs effectively.

In the hedge as we walked down to the huts, something in the grass made me jump; it was an injured young rook, dragging its wing and scuttling sideways through the long grass. I jumped, and the pony ignored it! You never know what they will spook at and that is what Matt is learning; whilst he should and can relax, he must still ride and not take his eye off the ball, the pony is young, and the rider needs to be vigilant.

Last weekend was Badminton Horse Trials and Matt went along to visit with his auntie, his grandma and his cousin. He did assure me that he was not taking Pandora with him, I must say that I was very relieved!

'The jumps were humungous, they were twice the height of Pandora,' said Matt, and the Shetland Grand National was brilliant and one jockey got bucked off. Sounds like the thrill and spills continue!

Chapter 5
First Lunging Session

When I arrived for Matt's lesson today, Lucy was walking alongside Matt and Pandora down the farm lane. I drove down the lane steadily. Matt's position was good and relaxed, his legs were stretching down nicely, heels down and shoulders relaxed; these are things that he is starting to do naturally. When we met up down in the yard, Philip went off to see if he could find some rope for a lunge rein, I have ordered a new one, but it will take a few days, my old one is beyond use. Matt stayed on the pony whilst his mum and dad looked for something appropriate to use. Pandora was a little edgy, she may have thought that was the sum of her ride for the day, she was keen to do more. Matt took her for a walk up the lane towards the house and then back down; they walked around the yard and the pony napped (misbehaved) a little when Matt tried to bring her back around. It was good to see this as I could support him by telling him to shorten and open his reins, use his outside leg and his voice to move her forward, she did a small jump in protest and Matt succeeded in bringing her around and back to where his dad and I were standing. These little episodes are all part of learning and re-enforcing positive behaviours with a pat when the pony has responded well. The rider also deserves a pat on the back for succeeding in his quest.

Lucy and Matt walked up the farm lane and I drove up ahead of them, the daffodils are noticeable only by their seed heads now and the red campion and herb robert (cranesbill family) are out along with buttercups, dandelions, wild garlic and a host of other wild flowers. The lambs, much bigger now, are still running and jumping along the hedge as I drive up. I park at the top and take the rope, the lunge whip and, of course, my gloves from the car and wait for the intrepid three to reach the top of the lane. We all walk down to the sand school.

Today the horses are still out in the fields and there is less distraction for pony and rider. The sand school is clear of poles and jumps which is a real bonus as we are beginning with lunging the pony for the first time. First time for us anyway, I assume that she will have been lunged previously, though that may be a big assumption.

We begin by crossing the reins and looping them around the stirrup leathers, stirrups up. I loop the lunge rope through the bit, to the off-side as we do not have a cavesson small enough. Pandora is a quiet pony and so I am not concerned that for today we do not have the "right" equipment. I will be very careful, and if I have any concern, I will stop immediately. The pony goes off at a trot initially and I let her do a couple of rounds, talking to her and telling her to trot, to re-enforce her pace. Very soon I can see she starts to listen, so I tell her to walk and she does "whoa" and she stops. We go off again at a walk and make a good transition to a trot at which point she gets a little excited and goes into a canter, with a small buck for good measure, I use my voice and she soon calms down and we work on the transitions and her listening to my voice. Once she is listening, I can explain to Matt what I am doing. It is good for him to see how she listens to the voice. I bring her to a halt again and do a couple of transitions walk-trot and trot-walk and halt. I tell her to stand, I walk over to her and change the lunge rope so that we can change the rein (go in the other direction). Like many ponies, she is not quite so relaxed or supple on the left rein, I wonder why that is, perhaps because for most of us it is easier to lunge on the right rein. I do not know the answer, though I have come across this before, many times, it must be the issue of clockwise and anti-clockwise. It did not help that at one point one of the dogs was chasing the end of my lunge whip, which was a little distracting!

I point out to Matt that Pandora is resisting the rein and looking to the outside of the circle putting here rump in. He notices that this looks different and I explain that if he was riding her, he would be using his outside leg just behind the girth and his inside leg on the girth to help her with the circle. As before, I am moving around the school with increasing and decreasing circles. I want the pony to get used to the school and she is still wary of the barrels in the corner, this way I can take her closer without it being threatening. The pony has a wall-eye, a blue eye on the left, does that affect her at all, I think not, but again I do not have a definitive answer; she is turning so that she can see the barrels with both eyes. We continue with the same process that we used for the right rein, this should help to balance her movements and in time working on both reins with help her to become supple. The pony did canter on both reins, and whilst this was not requested, she quickly came back down to a trot. Matt has not cantered her yet and so it was helpful for him to see that she has a good gentle canter and does not take off! In all, we lunged for twenty minutes, ten minutes on each rein, this is equivalent work to approximately an hour of hacking. Pandora was warm though she did not break out into a sweat. I was pleased with the result.

I removed the lunge rein, wound it up and put it, my gloves (always to be worn when lunging, just in case the pony pulls the rope through your hands) and my whip the other side of the gate. Lucy gave Matt a leg-up and he had a ride in the school. He walked on both reins and then did a couple of trots, also on both reins. Lucy and Matt laid out some poles so that he could do some trotting over them, for the pony they need to be paced at just under a metre apart. Pandora likes to follow people and so Lucy and I had to position ourselves to help Matt rather than to hinder. He needs to ride the pony and we also need to take into account what makes her feel safe at the age she is. Matt has a good handle on moving her forward, using his legs and his seat appropriately and to boost his confidence riding must be fun. Matt and the pony work well together and trot a circle around the poles and then over them on both reins a couple of times, after a slight difference of opinion to begin with. Including the riding up and down the farm lane, the pony has done about ninety-minutes work today and Matt feels he has done enough.

Lucy and I are happy with what the pony and Matt have achieved. It is very important to finish on a good note and so Matt and I walk back down the lane, the birds are still singing, and the church spire is just visible on the skyline. We put the pony in the stable, give her hay and water, bedding her down for a well-earned rest. The last time Matt rode, he took a tumble, this time he has succeeded in riding well and staying on top, correcting the pony when she napped, and he has seen the benefit of lunging. The pony has achieved, and so for both parties, we finish on a good point, and when we come back again, it will be with a positive attitude.

I will be away for next week and so I am putting a list together of what Matt can practise, all the things that he is already doing. This is not "homework", it is just a gentle reminder of everything he has already learnt. Tomorrow evening, he is attending a pony club event which I am sure will be great fun for both pony and rider. I am not in a mad rush to get Matt happily tearing around the fields or across the moors. I am taking pony and rider along at their own pace with regular time spent practising and perfecting what they know. A child of Matt's age would perhaps learn more from a schooled and older pony, we are working with what we have, a young inexperienced though very keen rider and the same of the pony and they are already building a great partnership. They have built a wonderful trusting relationship and this needs to be nurtured and progressed at their pace. Always finishing a session on a high, even when a tumble occurs, as it will sometimes. We all have tumbles and we need to get back on, forgive ourselves and the pony and get back to working together in a positive way with positive re-enforcement at the forefront of what we do.

When I return, we will hopefully be able to use the fields for lunging if they have finally dried out, and perhaps we will be able to have more use of the sand school if our neighbours agree. We are so lucky to have that as an opportunity.

Chapter 6
Safety Issues

I am away for just under a week, and the next time I see Matt, he is already tacked up. He did not want to go to the sand school today, just wanted to go along the lane to the shepherd's huts. As we went through the gate Matt was riding on ahead and I was concerned that he was moving too fast, given that he had taken a tumble when his pony had shied at the rubber matting previously. I stupidly did not shut the gate behind me as it needs tying up and I felt I needed to catch Matt up.

We went off down the lane, Matt trotting on ahead quite happily. We played a game, he had to ride between two blue buckets and so long as he completed the task, he could then ride up to me and collect a piece of chewing gum as a reward. This little exercise was to help when it came to pony club games such as handing a baton over, so it was about moving between two points and having to stretch in order to collect a small piece of chewing gum. With the handing the baton over in one of the games at pony club, the issue may have been the leaning forward and stretching, taking his seat out of the saddle perhaps making the pony feel unbalanced and therefore she pulled away. Perhaps the use of chewing gum helped as this was a successful game and brought smiles from rider, and the pony seemed quite happy with it all. Pandora had her treat later.

We continued with some good transitions from walk to trot and walk to square halt. It must seem strange to a child to hear that you push a pony into a halt, the natural thing would seem to be just stop pushing and it will stop! Having achieved some good halts, Matt made his pony walk two steps backwards and then walked forward again. Like the turn on the forehand, all of these moves are important for when pony and rider are confident enough to go and ride around the farm alone or check on the sheep and so on.

As we were heading back up the lane to return the pony to the stable, she started to trot very fast and Matt couldn't stop her. I called him and said, 'Sit back slightly, heels down, collect your reins and use your voice.' I used my voice as well, as I would if I were lunging. What was happening was that as soon as she started to trot of her own accord, Matt raised his seat, his toes went down and his hands went forward; as he regained his position, Pandora stopped trotting and he managed to bring her to a halt. Matt was a little shaken by the experience as was I, because I knew I had not shut the gate. We did a little more work so that we would complete the session on a good note and then we walked down to the stable. I praised Matt for his riding and I explained how stupid I had been about not closing the gate behind us. I explained why it is so important to close gates, especially with younger horses or ponies as they may get spooked by something and we need to make sure that both the rider and the pony are safe.

Matt was concerned that if the gate had been closed that she might have tried to jump it. I said I thought that very unlikely and that the gate would have made him feel safer, and by relaxing into his saddle, he had been able to stop her. She had become excited by the sound of the horses next door and thought she was going up to see them. Matt was feeling confident that he had stopped his pony and that he would be able to do so again. The session ended happily.

Once we had put Pandora safely in her stable, we took the tack up to the house and cleaned it together. We made quite a mess on the kitchen floor, but we managed to clean it all up before Lucy came home!

Chapter 7
Time to Canter

So far, summer 2018 has been wonderful for the sun worshippers and visitors to the county. For farms and gardeners though, whilst lovely for getting out and doing the work, the lack of water is taking its toll. Looking out towards Pentire Point as I write this, the land is scorched and bronzed, desperately thirsty. The days have been hot and the heat continuing until late into the evenings. No, I am not complaining, as I love the warmth of the sun, I have been walking the dogs on the moors where they can then swim in the rivers or we have taken them to the cove close by, Port Quin, where at low tide they can run on the sand and swim in the sea.

For Matt and Pandora, this wonderful weather has interrupted their routine. The heat has been too much sometimes for Matt to want to ride and I have to say whilst his pony loves the attention, she is quite happy ambling around her paddock until the sun begins to drop and the heat subsides. Then she goes into her cool stable overnight. However, the advantage of the dry ground is that the fields have been available for Matt to ride in. Lucy has taken Matt riding in one of the fields near the house, where there is a mound of sand and a mound of dung ready to be ploughed in to give added nutrients to the grass next year. Matt has been riding around the edge of the fields with Lucy close by, though not leading him. Like all ponies faced with a wide-open space, Pandora is a little edgy, frisky maybe, wondering just how much she can get away with in this space. The ground is so parched that she is not thinking of food, which is a change!

When I went over to the farm the other evening at about six o'clock, I met Matt and Lucy walking up the lane to the field. Off they went around the hedgerows and Pandora was getting quite excited, whilst Lucy walked with her, though she did not look to investigate her space too boldly. We need to always bear in mind here that we have a young pony and a young, keen though inexperienced rider. Matt was happy to ride off on his own and so I suggested that he might like to do some circles and figure of eights. This encourages both pony and rider to keep a focus on what they are doing and to keep the pony's mind off the potential galloping ground surrounding them both. I know that once Matt canters his pony, he will feel far more confident and will be looking to enjoy that space. For now, though, he is wanting to pace himself, his confidence is growing, and it would be wrong to push him too fast, though clearly challenge is good and moving the pace on is necessary, at the point when everyone is ready and able.

At first, the pony was not too keen on the idea of focus and circles and made Matt work for it, what became clear is that her young rider is very much in charge now and did not let the pony get away with anything. They circled and did some figure of eights using Lucy and me as markers, and Matt decided what he was going to do and when, he was also good at praising his pony. There is a great bond between these two. I really feel that Matt is ready to take the plunge into cantering now, he has cantered before, though not on Pandora, and once he starts, I am sure that he will enjoy himself, he will also be much better prepared for pony club during the summer holidays.

I have just read that the weather is on the change with hurricane Chris coming across the Atlantic, there will be some cooler days and some rain coming in at the weekend. The ground is extremely hard and perhaps a little rain will soften it enough to encourage Matt to take the plunge into cantering. We need to find a less open space for him, so that he feels safe and so that he can hear what is said to him, should he need some support or instruction. Perhaps he will ride this evening after school and we can do some preparation. Like his brother and sister, they are all very busy after school, with their various after-school clubs and they all love to help on the farm. In this wonderful weather, they frequently end the day with a swim at Port Quin with their dad, they have also been enjoying barbeques with cousins this summer. On top of that, of course, there is the ever-present homework and reading to be remembered!

The next day when Matt rode, Lucy and I had already decided that today is the day to move on to cantering. Matt and Lucy tack up Pandora who has already been bought in and treated with fly spray. We walk up to the field, where there is a tractor and dung spreader, not working, but being prepared for spreading tomorrow. Pandora is quite nonchalant about the machinery now, after her baptism of fire when she first arrived and then met Philip driving in the lane with the biggest load of round bales she had ever seen.

I had carried two blue buckets up to the field, and once the tractor left the field, Lucy and I pulled the gate across the entrance, for safety. I wanted Matt to work in the area near the lane, the mound of sand and dung was still there, so with the buckets, it made a cordoned off area from the expanse of the field. Matt started to ride around, Pandora was being very stubborn, and Matt was getting quite frustrated, however, once he was reminded to start with the basics, gather his reins, heels down, seat deep in the saddle and use his voice, off she went, helped by Lucy and me making all the right noises, this pony really listens to sounds. One of the horses from the neighbours whinnied and Pandora jumped forward, giving Matt a fright, though he stayed put, as he had geared himself up to get his pony moving forward again. Having done several good circuits around the set course, Matt changed the rein. Like many ponies, Pandora seems to move more fluidly on the right rein than the left and yet we always balance the work that Matt does with her. After working quite hard, Matt I mean, as the pony clearly thought the weather was a little muggy and not conducive to overdoing things, Matt said he thought they had done enough. I said there is one more thing that we are going to do and that is to canter. Matt is attending pony club on Friday after school and I want him to have at least experienced cantering with his own pony, before he attends.

Perhaps cantering on the lunge would have been more effective, though Matt preferred to do it by himself. He tried so hard, he rode his pony well, he geared up, sitting trot at the second bucket, turned to come up the field and no, the trotting became more powerful and Matt was using his legs well and had his heels down and his seat in a great position, second time lucky, no, third time lucky, oh so close, nearly there. Last time, and again, everything in place, Lucy even running alongside, pleased it was not me, and yes, yes, and no, not for lack of trying on Matt's part. He finished with a broad smile and patted Pandora hard on the neck saying, 'Good girl.' Whilst they had not achieved the canter, I think the fear of it has now dispersed, and as I said, when she does, both she and Matt will sit far more comfortably together. Perhaps more space would have clinched it, though remembering their combination, I still maintain that we need to progress at Matt's pace and not take unnecessary risks to achieve what are effectively, our own goals.

Lucy and I were pleased with how the twosome managed and how each time Matt became a little more confident and a little more in control. He is doing well and together they will do well at pony club on Friday.

On Thursday when I collect Matt and Dan from school, he excitedly shouts to his aunt, 'I nearly cantered.' He was so happy. Like all activities, some aspects are more fun than others and today I suggested that we cleaned the tack ready for the pony club event tomorrow. We took everything outside, the sun was shining, so perfect weather to do it all outside. Matt filled a bowl of water and took it outside with two scouring sponges. We took the bridle to pieces and I took the stirrups, leathers and girth off the saddle, talking through what I was doing to Matt. He was very conscientious and made a good job of cleaning, perhaps over soaped, though once cleaned off, everything looked good and he was pleased with his work. We washed the numnah and the girth in the washing machine, a bit different from cleaning the old string girths. I quite enjoyed myself, it's been a long time since I cleaned tack, it can be too easy to do everything for children, when they might quite enjoy the chores, so long as someone is helping them. My view is that if a child is old enough to have their own pony, they are old enough to take some responsibility. Matt took some pride in what he was doing and completed his task rather than making excuses and going off to do other things. He did ask me if I would catch Pandora and put her in the stable, to which I said no, that he could do it and it would be much nicer for the pony if he did it, as he owns her, rides her and loves her. It is not so much about capability as butterfly minds, children can always think of something else to do!

Chapter 8
Theory and Practice

Today I have read through what I have written so far and at this point I realise that Matt and Pandora have only been together for about fourteen weeks, they really are doing very well. Following the last lesson and nearly cantering, Matt is very keen to have a lesson on Monday to make sure that he does canter, so good news, onwards and upwards.

Well, between my lessons with Matt, he and Philip have been out in the twenty-acre field, Matt riding and Philip running! Together they cantered, briefly, but a canter all the same. The second attempt ended with a tumble, though Matt got straight back up and did not seem perturbed at all about trying again when I arrived to help him a couple of days later. So, Philip, Matt on Pandora, Lucy and I all traipsed down to the twenty-acre for a re-run of the previous cantering experience. I have to say that some of the young horses I have had in the past would have seen that open space and taken off whether I wanted to or not. Pandora, however, whilst energetic was very well behaved. Matt walked her down the field, trotted across the field and then when they were ready, Philip ran alongside Matt and his pony with the intention of cantering up the field Philip running fast, Matt used his legs and seat and had a good fast trot, though no break into canter. I said to Philip he would need to run faster! Three more attempts, a great deal of energy used and still she did not canter. She had, however, had plenty of exercise and Matt had worked really hard, Philip was ready for his supper and a well-deserved glass of beer.

I lunged the pony a couple of times this week and she performed well including in a canter, with a few bucks thrown in with the wind under her tail. Matt came and watched one evening and I asked him to shout out whether she was on the inside leg once she moved into a canter, I had explained what he needed to look for and we had talked about the leg movements in walk, trot and canter. The first couple of times he was incorrect, for the remaining times he was right every time. I think this is a great achievement for a seven-year-old's observation.

The ponies leg movements are quite different for each movement, or stride. Walk is a four-beat movement, right hind-leg leads, followed by right fore-leg, left hind-leg and finally left fore-leg. Trotting a two-beat movement where the left fore-leg moves forward with the right hind-leg and vice versa. Cantering is a three-beat movement. The right-lead Canter will be left hind-leg, then right hind-leg and left fore-leg, then right fore-leg. Left-lead Canter will be right hind-leg, then left hind-leg and right fore, then left fore-leg.

Whilst many people think that a gallop is a fast canter, the gait is in fact a four-beat movement. The right-lead gallop is left hind-leg, then right hind-leg, left fore-leg, right fore-leg. Left-lead gallop is right hind-leg, left hind-leg, right fore-leg and left fore-leg.

And, whilst we are on the subject of movement and leads, understanding the correct diagonal for trotting will also become important to Matt as he progresses. On the correct diagonal, you rise as the outside leg goes forward. So, trotting is being aware of the outside leg leading as you rise, and cantering is being aware of the inside leg leading.

You may be thinking that all this sounds very complicated for a seven-year-old child, however, by understanding the different strides and movements, it can help the rider to move with the horse and become more balanced. I remember my dad making a wooden model of a horse with wires attached to the four legs to show us which way the legs moved in each of the four movements and strides described. Matt may not completely understand this process at the moment, though he will come to understand it in time, and it will help him both with transitions and position.

When we had finished riding, Matt cleaned out the stable, Dan held Pandora whilst I pulled her mane to tidy her up ready for the pony club event at the weekend. All the family get involved and help, that is how it should be, as involvement and support encourages the rider, just as it does any sports person, whether it is Dan's rugby, or Beth's sailing.

Cousins and aunties also help with support and boosting confidence and for Matt, he is lucky enough to be able to ride out with his family. Thanks to the opportunity of riding with his cousin and auntie, Matt and Pandora have mastered the canter, there will be no stopping them now. Next lessons will be focusing on jumping, as during the holidays, pony club days have included small cross-country experiences, walking through water and going over poles and small cross-poles.

I am so pleased that Matt has been able to move at his own pace with his pony, he has become very keen and brave; his position is good, improving daily making him more secure in the saddle. Everything to go for now.

When I was looking after Matt, Beth and Dan last week, we were talking about jumping and I suggested to Matt that he designed a fantasy course for the field in front of this house. We would not be able to actually build the course as the fields are required for stock and we would actually only need a small area for practice jumps at this stage. I had initially made the suggestion because I had said 'no' to using the X Box and so needed to come up with another idea to keep them all busy!

The end result was well thought-out, somewhat ambitious, though supported by Beth also designing a course. Both courses involved cross bars, doubles and singles with fillers. Matt had considered the distances between the jumps and we had some discussion about the length of a stride, I think we may have to discuss this when we are actually out in the field with the pony. Bearing in mind that at this point we have no jumps!

I need to learn to keep quiet sometimes, as this has led me to ordering two types of uprights and cavaletti blocks along with a load of pipes from our local building supplies shop. Beth has ideas for cutting up a telegraph pole and jig-sawing some wood and painting panels. As I said we do have to ask Philip, their dad, before we commandeer one of the fields! Naturally, farmers do not want fields cut up from ponies careering around and sliding into jumps. Following this incredibly dry summer, grass is in short supply and so is at a premium for the stock.

The jumps and pipes have arrived this week, I ordered pipes as they can be painted, and they are much lighter to carry around. The uprights are short and again light enough to be moved around the field, brought inside during the winter and yet heavy enough to stand up when knocked.

Whilst I have been writing these last few lines, Matt has been on the telephone, saying that he and Philip have put the jumps together and could I go over after lunch and help him ride over them, I asked him what he thought of them as I have not seen him, he said, 'They're alright.' I hope that they are more than just alright, though I guess at this point for Matt they are just jumps!

Having been summoned to help Matt with his jumps, I drove over to the farm about 4.30pm thinking that I could get the jumps up and ready before he came home from the other farm with his dad. I had received a second call saying could I change the time until 5pm as Matt wanted to go off with his dad in the afternoon. The weather had improved from this morning's drizzle. This was good, and the ground was soft, though not wet, and the pony will benefit from that as she does not have shoes. It was still misty and low cloud when I left, I could not see Pentire Point or the sea through the mist.

Lucy and I had a cup of tea and a chat before Matt arrived home, we could not put the jumps out as we were unsure which field Philip would want us to use. As it happened, we used the field closest to the house, the same one that Matt had designed his fantasy course for. We did, however, use the rectangle near the shed as this gave three sides of boundaries for both the pony and Matt.

I set the cavaletti blocks up with just a stride between so

that the pony could trot over these, this was just under a metre as she has quite a short stride, she is only 11.2hh. Having set the blocks, I dropped the pipes onto the ground for a starting point. The two uprights were set side by side with a few metres between. Both uprights had cross poles and the uprights pulled wide so that the level was low. None of these jumps were higher than Matt has already ridden over. Due to his success in taking the pony over the poles, where Pandora picked her feet up beautifully, and the two jumps, I was able to increase the cavaletti blocks to the first and then the second level. The cross-poles stayed on the jump that followed the cavaletti and the other was put to a straight pole and a ground pole so that it could only be ridden

There were a couple of run-outs, though I have to say that Matt managed Pandora beautifully, he used his voice, his legs, lightly used the whip, but was not relying on it. It is important that the reins are kept short enough to have constant contact with the pony and this is something that we need to work on so that the pony does not see an opportunity to run out. Having said that, there is a great deal to think about and to co-ordinate in order to complete these jumps, added to which there was an audience of five people.

I tried to encourage Matt to watch me as he came towards the jumps as it is very easy to lose focus, and in looking in the wrong direction, it is possible to give the pony a different message about where to go. It is an idea sometimes to ask the child to count how many fingers you hold up so that they concentrate on their direction of travel. Pandora is very sensitive to her rider's movements and this focus helped Matt to look ahead between the pony's ears.

On the last round of Matt wanting to complete the jumps again, the pony ran out at the last minute and took her rider by surprise, he came off on to the upright. However, he was feeling so keen about his jumping he got straight back up and when I asked if he wanted me to turn it into a cross-pole again, his answer was, 'No, I'll just do it again.' And he did, in fact he did the whole course and a clear round. I am hoping that this success will take him through a great day at pony club camp tomorrow.

A successful evening and a very happy rider, a praised pony and Matt's comment, 'I have the best pony ever, I really love her.'

Chapter 9
Pony Club Cross-Poles

Matt and Pandora enjoyed a busy summer with several pony club events. Last week, and prior to Matt having his own jumps set up, I went along to the cross-poles event with Philip and Lucy to see how the intrepid twosome were getting on. I was interested to see how Pandora reacted with the other ponies and to see how Matt managed within a group. Matt gets on well with people, I just wondered how he would manage the pony, given that most of their riding at home is just the two of them, except for the occasions when he goes and rides with his cousin and aunt.

It turned out to be an eventful morning. Philip parked the horse-box, Lucy unloaded the pony and Matt started riding around the field with other riders. Pandora was energised, Matt managed well, keeping her interested and moving on. We then walked down a concrete track towards the riding area, there were three groups of riders, different ages and different ability. It took me back to my days of teaching at pony club, it seems like another life-time now. As we all walked down the lane, there was a bit if a kafuffle and I saw

Matt standing on the ground and Lucy calming Pandora. The lane had electric fencing both sides and it was linked with a covered wire across the lane. The covering on the wire across the lane had corroded and shorted the wire, Pandora had received a shock as she walked over it, thankfully she had no shoes on and recovered quickly. Matt was left feeling a little shaken. The electric was turned off and the owner was apologetic. Clearly, the other ponies and horses had all walked over safely. You could hear the shorting easily from the loud clicking sound.

On a personal note, I was pleased to be walking nearer the back as I have a pace-maker fitted for my heart and whilst I have had my heart shocked through cardioversion at the hospital on several occasions, this kind of shock could have caused the pace-maker to reset and make things difficult.

We all walked on down to a small meadow at the bottom and the other two groups went off with their instructors. Today was very much about jumping small cross-poles and taking ponies through water which formed part of a very good cross-country course which some of the older and more experienced riders were enjoying. There were four children in Matt's group, I think Pandora was the youngest pony and Matt possibly the youngest rider. Matt brought up the rear of the ride, given this is a relative novel experience they managed well. They had a walk around the meadow, followed by a trot and then went through two jump posts over trotting poles. Pandora is very interested in her surroundings and does find it difficult to keep her focus on the pony in front of her. Matt found it difficult on occasions to keep up with the pony in front and perhaps also struggled to focus on the immediate job in hand, he was perhaps dreaming of thundering across the field and over the cross-country jumps!

There were three areas of the course for Matt's group and they enjoyed the opportunity to jump over low cross-poles. There were occasions when both Pandora and another pony refused (avoided the jump), though both came back and did complete the jumps. As the instructor said to Matt, Pandora is very young and very supple, this does make it a little more difficult for Matt than riding a schooled and older pony who is quite happy with straight lines. The second set up of jumps were around a clump of trees and all of the group really enjoyed this, and despite a couple of run outs, they all succeeded and were happy with their achievements. They would all have liked to take another turn at this set, unfortunately, the older group wanted to move on to these jumps and so there was no time; this was a shame as a second run would have boosted the confidence of this younger group. We trekked back up the hill where there were three more jumps and on the way the riders took their ponies through the water. Pandora made Matt work hard, she did the jumps and the water, though she was not going to make it easy for her rider! As we started up the hill, some of the older riders were going full-pelt through part of their cross-country at the bottom of the field and this spooked several of the ponies causing a tumble for one child and scaring a couple of the others including Matt. This was very unfortunate and unnecessary because at this point, they were all keen to have a crack at this new set of jumps, having enjoyed the previous set. Unfortunately, whilst they did all jump the last set, they had lost their enthusiasm and were wary of the older group who were galloping through and around the area where the younger group were supposed to be jumping.

It is difficult when you have three mixed groups with limited space and opportunity for trying new things. It seems that it may have been better to have had the younger group on a different day or perhaps two groups in the morning and two groups in the afternoon to make better use of the space. The facility was good and a great opportunity for people to practice and hone their cross-country riding. Despite the tumble for a couple of the riders, the morning was generally enjoyed and what is remembered is what you liked and what you jumped. The children were riding for about an hour and three-quarters and it was quite intense, watching, listening, observing others and concentrating on your own riding and pony. I think everyone was quite tired by the end of the session and ready to go home.

From my perspective, it was useful for me to see Matt perform in the group situation with his pony, as this is not something I have witnessed before. I noticed that he was quite relaxed, that he is more confident and that being in the group reduces the tension and focus being just on him. He still loses concentration sometimes, though he is buoyed up by the group. Seeing pony and rider in a different light will help me to give him support in the areas that he really needs, and so, as I have said before, flatwork and jumping will be our focus. The pony needs the flatwork as she needs the schooling, her rider also needs the schooling and like all of us will look forward to the icing on the cake which for Matt will be the jumping. Having observed and listened to the pony club instructor, I can see where I need to offer support and help in between these types of events.

Chapter 10
Jumping Mania!

Matt having his own jumps has, as I had hoped, made him very keen to ride, and I would agree that it is so much more exciting to jump than to just concentrate on flatwork. We do, however, need to work hard on the flatwork, to ensure that Matt is secure in his saddle and does not come off a cropper as we might say! At this time, he is very keen, determined and appears to have little fear, he is a brave rider. Whilst this is good both for his confidence and the pony, we, or I, need to remember that both are still inexperienced and young.

It is about five months since Matt first met Pandora, the pony of his dreams. They have a wonderful close relationship; can both be stubborn and a bit nappy, and together are a great team. They trust each other and there is a lot to be said for that in pony and rider partnerships.

We have added to the jumps by including some rectangular buckets and we change the format frequently, neither pony nor rider should become over familiar with the jumps, they should use the same amount of care, planning and negotiation no matter how many times they jump together. For now, we are working on spread rather than height; at least until I feel Matt is secure.

There was amazing courage, determination and hard work this afternoon. Pandora was being a little stubborn and nappy, though Matt overcame that and pushed her forward. The pony loves people and she gravitates towards anyone who is standing nearby, so to help to keep her going I have to keep on the move as well. We succeeded with a clear round after one or two knocks, no refusals though. The jumps were low and had a little stretch, not too much. From the rider's perspective he had to keep working as I put three cavalletti on a curve that led into a cross bar, followed by a single bar set on its own. We then moved some of the jumps and made a broad one from

two cavelletti and a single at the beginning. Next time, we will work on style and position I think as we have had flappy reins, flappy legs and flappy stick today, though we have also had a lot of smiles, satisfaction and a happy pair, pony and rider.
I can see a great deal of daylight between the seat and the saddle during cantering, understandable as this is new to them both, heels need to be down in order to keep the seat down and the legs in the correct position. I have bought some training reins, they have different colours, these are great, as Matt can remember which colour he should be holding for cantering, trotting and jumping. There is so much to remember that all these aids to simplify are great for beginners and especially children, who are trying to remember so many different instructions.
For now, it is important to get the flow, between pony and rider, transitions and position are all important. Relaxation is also important, though too much confidence and relaxation can be potentially unsafe, and this is something I have become increasingly aware of with Matt. He is so relaxed with his pony; he looks as though he could quite easily just slide off her back!
Following a very good, mostly jumping, session on Tuesday, despite the fact we had planned to do flatwork. We have decided that the next lesson, possibly Saturday afternoon, will definitely, maybe, mostly be flatwork. It has been the first week back to school following the summer holidays and whilst Matt would not admit to it, I expect he is quite tired. Saturday afternoon will be the best time for a lesson as the return to school does rather wear children out, getting back to all their routines and after school clubs, unless he already has plans!
I will be collecting some leaves for the next session to try to show Matt how he needs to sit down in the saddle when doing a walk, sitting trot and canter. Children always want to succeed, and he will be no different, he will try very hard not to lose the leaves, and even more so if the reward is a couple

of small jumps to end the session. We all need to have ideas up our sleeve and grannies are no different to any other instructor.

Chapter 11
Maggie Arrives

Great excitement. Pandora is going to have a friend. Maggie is coming to stay!

Matt loves hacking when he has the opportunity, though this generally comes about when his aunt has time, along with his cousin, to meet up and go out together. Everyone is so busy with so many different responsibilities and, of course, the children, all needing to be taxied in opposite directions for their various sports, friends and activities.

Now, however, Matt will have more opportunity to hack out, with company. Sadly, for me, Maggie is not big enough for me to ride, she is a Dartmoor pony and whilst quite stocky and strong I think my legs would be dangling around her knees. Whilst that may be amusing to see, it would not be practical, I think it could become quite a tangle.

I have a feeling that both Lucy and grandad will be involved more than ever now. Grandad is a retired National Hunt jockey and is just the right size, though I am sure he will feel huge on Maggie, who after all is a pony, and Lucy is fine for riding her. Both ponies are moving to a new home and coming over to live in the field in front of my house. The field is to be separated off with electric fencing, suitable for ponies, the white tape that they can easily see. It is unlikely to need to be switched on as they will have ample grass is each area. Pandora, of course, may manage to slip underneath if she happens to be grazing below, she is a cheeky pony and definitely has a mind of her own. There are two good size stables in the yard, where we kept our own horses and ponies when we were children. Pandora won't know herself in such luxury.

The moving means, of course, that Matt will not be able to just amble down to the yard and visit Pandora when he feels like it and that is a shame; the plus side, however, is that they will be able to ride out together, which will be good for

Pandora. It is easy to forget how young she is, rising five now, and she really needs to hack and see some more of the big wide world. Whilst she is very used to big farm machinery, she has not a great deal of experience with cars and vans that may be heading towards her or sneaking up behind her when she is not looking. These will be new experiences for the intrepid duo. At the farm where Pandora was living, the roads are really not very safe, there is fast and sometimes heavy traffic. So far, the weather has been very wet, the fields are sodden and ponies racing around would only cut up the ground.

Matt will come over with Lucy every, well mostly, mornings to put the ponies out, skip out (remove the dung) the stables and then change and go on the school. Returning after school to bring the ponies in and to ride when the weather permits.

Today as I am writing this, I cannot even see the ponies in the field the mist is thick, and the constant rain would make it unsafe to ride along the lanes. We are surrounded by typical Cornish lanes, high hedgerows, sharp corners and, at this moment, plenty of surface water. Visibility is not good at the best of times, though when it is clear and dry or even drizzle, it is possible to hear oncoming cars and be able to pull into the hedge or a gateway. At the moment, it is not easy to decipher the sounds of running water, rain, wind and sounds carried from the main road or even planes and helicopters.

I can remember once, many years ago when I was riding my horse down the lane passed the Quaker burial ground, it was an Autumn day, good light and clear visibility. I heard this terrible rumble of a noise coming up behind me and assumed it was a tractor and trailer or a lorry. My horse was quite young, Bentley he was called. I turned to see what was coming and could see nothing, and as I looked, two jet aircraft shot out of nowhere and over our heads. Neither Bentley nor I had time to react or be scared, it happened so quickly,

So, so loud though.

My dad used to say that when out riding, it was good to look over the hedges and see what other farmers were doing in their fields. Sometimes you can see where vehicles are coming from, not always though. It is important to do a mental risk assessment before going out riding. We cannot foresee everything and there are certain risks, as with most sports, that is part of it. The important thing is to keep safe and to enjoy what you are doing. The awareness of risk is good, it keeps us on our toes.

So, let us see how Matt and Pandora, along with Maggie, progress from here. In their first nine months, Matt and Pandora have had so much fun, learnt a great deal, become firm friends and are now ready to move on to the next step. Matt is so lucky, he has his whole family supporting, helping, encouraging him with his riding. Everyone has something a little bit different to offer him and so he gains knowledge and information, that he then has, to keep, to practise or to discard. That is, after all, how we all learn.

Chapter 12
Pandora and Maggie, New Challenges

Maggie arrived mid-November and both, she and Pandora, have moved into their stables, and are enjoying the field in front of my home. I am so lucky to have a view of the sea, Pentire Point, the sheep in the fields, my ducks and our chickens in the garden and now the ponies in the field.

Philip, Lucy and the children are away for a couple of days and so my job is to look after the ponies. In the mornings, the ponies go out in the field, I muck out the stables and bed them up ready for the evening, with hay, fresh water and ample bedding. It is good to spend some time with both ponies, to observe their behaviours and the pecking order.

Maggie is the boss!

I think that Matt is struggling a little with the change of environment and the weather, he had such a great summer riding and doing things with Pandora. We have collected his jumps and Lucy brought them over in the truck, these will be inside for the winter in the hope that they will last longer than being left out in the wet fields. They could do with a coating of wood-preservative.

Lucy and grandad met Matt at school today, grandad riding Maggie and leading Pandora and Lucy drove to collect Matt and help him change ready to ride home. A very short distance of road for this ride which will then bring them through the golf course home. Not riding across the golf course. There will be some traffic, though little compared to the lanes.

My younger sister, Clare, has also started to help as well by riding Maggie and leading Pandora, so she is getting exercise and getting used to the regular traffic around the lanes. Matt is lucky to have a choice of three people now to collect him from school with his pony, not a bad life. With the time of the year and the weather, where to ride is limited and, of course, the dark evenings don't help, so riding home from school a couple of times a week is great. Matt is getting used to riding on the roads and both he and Pandora are building in confidence. It helps having Maggie, who is about twelve years of age and far more experienced, and she is quiet to support Pandora.

Pandora does seem to get tired easily and what we have come to see is that Matt sadly is outgrowing her. Pandora has been part of the family for almost a year now and has taught Matt a great deal. She has a beautiful temperament and is willing to learn. Matt will move on soon, perhaps to Maggie and Pandora will be sold and given a new home and opportunity to help another child to ride and enjoy her company. It is always a sad day when ponies have to move on, the important thing is to keep the great memories and make sure that her next owner is as right for her as she is for them. Due to her size, Pandora may have multiple owners, except perhaps if there are two or three children who will come to enjoy her in one family. Pandora is a more knowledgeable pony now than she was when she came to Matt, she is very affectionate, more used to traffic and roads, has attended pony club and is ready to help another child to fulfil their dreams.

Matt's legs will need to grow a little more in order to ride Maggie in the way that he has ridden Pandora. Maggie has experience and they seem to get on well together, she is a little big for Matt just at the moment. They have already attended pony club events where both Pandora and Maggie have gone with Matt and he has spent some time with both of them. It has been an interesting year supporting Matt and Pandora. They have progressed well together. The winter weather has hindered more recent progress, though now that the clocks have gone forward and we have more daylight, riding is easier again. We have come full circle, back to lambing time and Easter holidays. When Matt is unable to ride, I try to lunge Pandora so that she keeps up her fitness, it is clear that Matt is now beginning to outgrow her and she lets him know when she has had enough, by refusing to move!

It will soon be time for the advert to go out, so that Pandora continues her learning and fun with a new owner. Matt will miss her terribly, he may well see her at pony club, being ridden by her new owner. Matt will eventually move on to Maggie, and then, will Lucy find something else for her, perhaps a horse that is big enough for me to ride as well? We shall see. Pandora has matured so much recently and muscled up, so we may hang fire with the advert until the end of the summer. Matt and Pandora are enjoying the light evenings, riding around the lanes and attending pony club events. The more that they do now, the more experienced Pandora will be for a new, slightly younger rider next year. It is interesting to see how Pandora has matured over the last year, she is now five years old and far more experienced about life, including having become very used to the traffic around our narrow lanes. Sometimes, time is the most important factor for children and ponies alike. We all need time to acclimatise to new experiences and situations.

Pony Club is a wonderful organisation to help children and their ponies to learn and to socialise with like-minded people. The opportunities include, teaching, cross-country and show-jumping and, of course, all important, making new friends and having a great deal of fun.

Matt attended Badminton three-day event again with his auntie and cousin last weekend and, again, thoroughly enjoyed himself. He is in awe about the size of the jumps and having watched the Shetland racing again has decided that is on his to-do list! Badminton itself will have to wait for a while.

Will we get a horse that both Lucy and I can ride in the future, who knows? The main thing is that Matt is on his way as a more confident rider, enjoying himself and making friends, that is what it is all about. The more time that Matt spends around horses, the more confident he becomes. He has even driven a carriage with four beautiful Gelderlander horses, along the lanes with six people as passengers, this was his eighth birthday present experience. He loved it. Naturally, Will was sitting beside him ready to take the reins if required.

Matt has an affinity with horses and ponies, he is gentle on the bit and rides with compassion. He has been invited to go and help with the driving horses during the summer holidays.

Pony club season is underway again and there is an event on Sunday. When we took Pandora into the field to do some jumping yesterday, she was quite excitable. I will start lunging her again, so that she has a little more regular exercise and that will help Matt when he wants to go in the field and ride. I really would like to get a horse myself so that I can perhaps support Matt a little bit more and also save Lucy some time, by riding out with Matt myself.

So, watch this space, will Matt continue his enthusiasm for riding, it certainly suits him and is a very therapeutic past time. Will he one day, perhaps, find a career with horses or will he simply continue to enjoy them as a hobby?

The End